BLINDSIGHT

The Book of Shares by Edmond Jabès (Chicago University Press)
The Book of Margins by Edmond Jabès (Chicago University Press)
The Little Book of Unsuspected Subversion by Edmond Jabès
(Stanford University Press)
Some Thing Black by Jacques Roubaud (Dalkey Archive)
The Plurality of the World According to Lewis by Jacques Roubaud
(Dalkey Archive)
Late Additions by Emmanuel Hocquard (*Série d'Ècriture #2*)
Dawn by Joseph Guglielmi (*Série d'Ècriture #5*)
The Vienna Group: Six Major Austrian Poets
(with Harriet Watts, Station Hill)
Paul Celan: Collected Prose (Carcanet / Sheep Meadow)
With Each Clouded Peak by Friederike Mayröcker
(with Harriet Watts, Sun & Moon Press)
Heiligenanstalt by Friederike Mayröcker (Burning Deck: *Dicten=#1*)
Mountains in Berlin: Selected Poems by Elke Erb
(Burning Deck: *Dicten=#2*)
Where Are We Now by Peter Waterhouse (Duration Press)
A Test of Solitude by Emmanuel Hocquard
(Burning Deck: *Série d'Ècriture #12*)
Many Glove Compartments by Oskar Pastior (with Harry Mathews and
Christopher Middleton, Burning Deck: *Dichten=#5*)

ESSAY

Against Language? (Mouton / Walter de Gruyter)
Lavish Absence: Recalling and Rereading Edmond Jabès
(Wesleyan University Press)

ROSMARIE WALDROP

BLINDSIGHT

A NEW DIRECTIONS BOOK

The author would like to thank The Lila Wallace–Reader's Digest Fund
for a Writer's Award.

Grateful acknowledgment is made to the editors and publishers of magazines and anthologies in which parts of this book first appeared: *American Letters & Commentary, Arshile, Bombay Gin, Chicago Review, Columbia Poetry Review, Conjunctions, Crone's Nest, Denver Quarterly, Fence, The Germ, Hardpressed Poetry: The Journal, Hotel Amerika, Inscape, The Iowa Review, Mirage #4Period(ical), New American Writing, NO, Phoebe, Proliferation, The Prose Poem, Ribot, Seneca Review, Sulfur, Syllogism, Untitled,* and the anthology *A Convergence of Birds,* ed. Jonathan Foer (New York: D.A.P., 2001).

Chapbooks have been made of "Blindsight" (Saratoga, CA: Instress, 1998) and "Cornell Boxes" (Los Angeles: Seeing Eye Books, 2001).

Major sources are: Hölderlin; Yoel Hoffman, *Bernhard*; Richard J. Herrnstein and Edwin G. Boring, eds., *A Source Book in the History of Psychology*; Angela Carter, *Saints and Strangers*; Hans Reichenbach, *The Philosophy of Space and Time*; and Dore Ashton, *A Joseph Cornell Album.*

Book design by Sylvia Frezzolini Severance
Manufactured in the United States of America
New Directions Books are printed on acid-free paper.
First published as New Directions Paperbook 971 in 2003
Published simultaneously in Canada by Penguin Books Canada Limited

Library of Congress Cataloging-in-Publication Data

Waldrop, Rosmarie.
  Blindsight / Rosmarie Waldrop.
    p. cm.
  ISBN 0–8112–1559–8 (pbk.: alk. paper)
  I. Title.
PS3573.A4234B55 2003
811'.54—dc21
                                    2003010671

New Directions Books are published for James Laughlin
by New Directions Publishing Corporation,
80 Eighth Avenue, New York, NY 10011

FOR C.D. WRIGHT

CONTENTS

HÖLDERLIN HYBRIDS

FOR CHARLES BERNSTEIN

I. IN A DOORWAY

FOR LISA JARNOT

1

The world was galaxies imagined flesh. Mortal. What to think now? Think simple. Matter? A lump of wax? An afterglow? Or does everything happen of its own accord? Perfect and full-bodied. No more. Observable. No longer. In your eyes or line of sight. Down all three dimensions of time. Or lock up the house. Or prophets.

▲

Here I work toward. A kind of elegy. Here a strange ceiling. "Earth fills his mouth." I would look at you. And write you. A spell but slack at the edge. And in the door where I stand your voice goes. Hollow.

▲

If what happened. (Happened?) Hand. Between palms. Grief. Death. Coffee with cream. Coffee. Arms, knees and free will. And shiny. Rainbows.

▲

The words have detached. And spread throughout my body. Such reckless growth. Windbag! Want to see come full circle the wheel? To comment. My own commentary till I till. My own great-granddaughter's body?

▲

Absence. But it cuts. Repeat. Furiously Yes then No. Even a fictional character catches a chill. Makes the heart. And cold penetrates. We do not fall off the surface. But you, planet earth. Grow. Even as we read. Fonder of the dark.

2

Electric bulb. How the words are. Suspended around you. And. Bones in the body.

▲

In packets comes the voice. Often have I emptiness, it says. Emptiness is enough and as good as within. If your own strength carries your bones let emptiness. Lift them up to the sky. Often have I attempted the sky but it hears me not. The way corollaries are and the air. Transparent. Or not. Head wrapped in fog. But always always the earliest memory. Comes. Not as light but sluggishly. More visible must. More like a weather vane must memory. Then it revolves in feeling. In pubic hair. As if taking place.

▲

Grass grows. But stalagmites too rise from below. Else out of order the world. And the more blurred, the more lost in thought. That water rises as the pipes burst we understand. Which is why the need and power to see an oak and think "oak." Is given us. And transparent flesh. And the eye, most dangerous of lenses, is given. So that we should see and imagine and think and be out of the question. So that we might weigh our answers with scales. From our eyes fallen.

▲

Nowhere among the living. He remains. No razor gathers.

▲

Strange things happen and unexpected. Not that I to you. Want to expose myself. And flesh touching flesh cannot explain. Innumerable cells. Spreading inward.

3

Something else it is. To leave your house and cross the
Atlantic, Mediterranean, Aegean, Pacific. So many were
killed. And to stand each. In a doorway. And say I don't
live here.

▲

In the dark leaf nerve fibers spread out and from the brain.
Scatter and like flames. From the spinal cord. Stinging.
And stimuli from every. By ravenous hunger overcome.
Transmitting backwards and forwards. "Nerves" more than
seven. Dwarfs hi ho off to work. And farewell to the per-
sonal. Pronoun.

▲

So Mohammed. Rinaldo. Barbarossa. As divided into frag-
ments. The emperor Heinrich. I am however mixing up
the centuries. But gloom there is. In every needle, thread,
and cloth. Crossed the Alps and with his own voice sighed
"some things . . . " And his son Konrad of poison died.
Hark ye the horn of the watchman at night. And hair. Away
from the body grows.

▲

Tendons. Muscles. Sweat. Interrupt their conversation. A man. A man by the sea. A woman. The earth and its inhabitants. Antigone. Antibody. Anathema. Discrimination, fine. What is a body? Moves. Passes water. Again and again.

▲

When above the poem flames. And coal black the dream. Round the soles of your feet because. The earth pulls your body. More fiery through spheres plunged. But lovely it is the soul to unfold. And the sand burning.

4

The moon is a thin line and we see a thin line.
By Thebes and thieves! let not our names be blotted out.

▲

The things that enter one's skull. But a real skeleton. With
key. And describing your eyes the dark.

▲

Plainly a heavy heart. Can it bring about death?
Impossible to understand. But when heavy the feet yet
venture out. On a path you know as long. As you live you.
Cannot die.

▲

A horse stares unblinking. You slap a tree trunk as if. To
imprint all that's the case. Or a snow goose high above the
globe. Where are you?

▲

Stripes. Blue lilies. You know your neck. (Not your mind.)
Is damp with sweat. And like the more solid vase both. Not
without limits.

5

Narcissus, clematis, ranunculus, rancor. All the forces of flesh. And spirit clash. Shrieking birds inside your body. As when you say both Yes and No instead of music. To your own questions. As if flesh were not. Grass death should forget to mow. The ship anchored. In your head goes up. In flames and time backwards.

▲

You should take everything. Except your shoelaces. To heart. Which moves within the flesh. And should.

▲

My friend. Take care not to die. Not be torn to pieces. And let not because we're raw. Gods lash with waves our flesh. And its muscles and fibers and vessels and fat. And with this spell move on. If indeed life is. A dream it had better be. A good one. Which goes to the heart. Yet the world is all air. My luck to hear scholars debate the word "smoke" and not. Suffocate. Whereas imaginings take shape. As though in this world.

II. IN EARLY NOVEMBER

1

Penetrates to the bones. The cold. Inside which marrow.
Over which we must a woolen blanket spread. Another
person's body should lie. On yours and upside down the
sun. But in the wind crows. The vane.

▲

When down the stairs. And think "I'll make tea" or "Why
is our happiness steeped in longing?" As if they were the
same. A little darker then. So isolated in the mind a
human figure. Sail boat. Elephant.

▲

Mind's eye if concealed. Knife if sharpened. If I were a fig-
ment in somebody's head the pain could not be. This
strong. Let not darkness fall. On the space of missing

memory. Hard is it. To fill with lemons. With children too.
Just air.

▲

The windows the bells ring through. As if gates. Because
still modeled on nature, on trees, the gates. And autumn
wind. The image of the moon in water. Has been blown
away. Out of all the molecules and atoms rise higher and
higher buildings. Muting the air.

2

Movement however. How does it come? Do I think I'll spread my legs before I spread my legs? Whom (whose legs) do I imitate? May a woman. From the mess of her life look up and say: let me be. Like the heroine in a novel?

▲

As long as her legs are covered with fine hair and rain. Falls mixed with hail. Her ankle measures up against any Albertine, Anna, Hester, Molly, Dorothea, Emma, Sonja, Natasha, and Mme. Chauchat. Is only herself a woman? Is manifest as a view of trees her nature? Is she hiccuping?

▲

Iron rail. Of thumb. Not to stumble where your boldest. Dreams stand between.

▲

Such is the sight of the sea. Reverses time. And he thought he'd only have to cry "Mother." Under water. And his love. No purer a tango in the starry night, if I may say. Than his purpose to hold close her body.

▲

Is there love on earth? Difficult to think about. What is deep inside. But lovely the envelope of the body. Because it envelops. I discover late in life the ancients. Had already studied diseases of skin.

3

To bleed in body and heart and fall among particles. Does this please the Gods? The Angel of Death is abroad. The soul I believe must leave its house in the morning lest. Howling dogs cavort among orifices. And the voice of. So many birds.

▲

In a major key: dear old body how you pass. In August. From one year to another. Like a telescope through the Milky Way. I know you well but a sharp pain cuts. Through my stomach. And sinks like a stone down to the bottom. And is not an idea. And the moon I see enter the window. I don't without good reason compare. Floods the plain.

▲

This I know. The scales flash silver under the knife and the pike. Ceases to think. And Heine is covered with the Hebrew for blanket. But my body aches from. The mare I ride through the night. In my dream we did not sit together.

▲

Butterflies however fluster me. As they flutter. Almost unreal. All my desires it is true. Are presumptuous. Would I like to be a comet? They are swifter than birds and flower in fire. But skin is only external. And one thing touches another. More than air moves about in waves.

4

Of the sound that fills space. To capture. More than the tiniest part is beyond. Our ears though they stick. Out from the skull. On the other side of the wall a tapping. A knife on wood? Followers of materialism believe matter. Is solid. Lifeless lumps of clay in the field. Others, that even a stone's not simple. And of movement the source not external but found? In matter itself?

▲

Ethereal matters dissolve in particle and wave. Body fluids feed. Flushed. What was her name? Blackbird. Birth. Bath. Wherever we go we carry. Our male or female organs.

▲

When a man looks in the mirror and sees his soul. As an image. Is it a kind of insect? A thing with wings, three pairs of legs, two antennae? But if a man's eyes are closed when he dies. Will the soul burst? Through the skin? King Oedipus had an eye too many. The suffering of this man. Was it spiritual or only indescribable?

▲

When a play such a thing represents. How do I feel? Or thinking of you? A fact carried away by: The world is big and wide? As if I didn't understand that everyone dies. Can we avoid error? If we speak clearly and to the point? His suffering of course. Oedipus had that.

▲

But I want no more to pray. With inner organs. Too long to long. To lust. And drawers for first things first. And shoes.

5

To have it cut open. Your chest. And your flesh peered at and operated. This is pain. But it also is suffering when with a rash is covered red a woman. And crows stare at her with one eye.

▲

This is the work of the light. It breaks up and divides into colors. Yet impossible to see inside the body. To liver, gall bladder, kidney, spleen, intestines. To the suffering of Oedipus that moves upon the face of the fluids. Without form. And void. And darkness is upon the son of Laios.

▲

And afterwards as in a kind a nightmare. Desires are gathered together unto one place. And a city appears.

III. EVENING SUN

1

On a balcony onto the Seekonk stands. And full of
thoughts of winter. My friend. And drunk with red wine I.
Think of the power. Of a single word. Like for example
"fact." When I know what matters. Is between.

▲

But how with gnarled hands hold the many and how? The
sun and shadow of Rhode Island? Let alone the earth?

▲

Down swoops the hawk. From the sky over Providence.
The sky over my head. Down to the leaves inward curled
on the ground. But not like buds. Yellow. A cat is buried
here and the leaves. Swirl up in the wind.

▲

In the hour of the hawk. What is meant by: I think? Or even: I sit under clouds in which. Rain gathers weight. I sit in my mother's shawl which is. Threadbare. In my head I sit. By the river Euphrates. Strange like water the skies of the dead.

▲

And high from the branches of the maple. Like a prelude to snow. White feathers.

2

But music. Quickens the house down into its shadows. So trembles air in the sun and the shape of the tree blurs as if through a flame seen. Swarms of monarch butterflies stir and brush your cheeks. In celebration. In memory.

▲

Almost visible the words of the song. Leave the singer's mouth and rise up into the sun. Which goes crazy instead of down.

▲

Floods, storms, fires. But a tank won't be stopped by a word. Not even if you shout it from the middle of the road, with hands thrown forward and fingers spread out.

▲

Nor by music. Though its power is great. Like the heat of noon it slants between body and soul. Difficult, then. Unaccustomed as we are to beauty. To know which is effect and which cause.

▲

Not merely as a sailor is present in a ship am I. In my body. Intermingled.

3

My father thought he had the gift to read the stars. To know if the light in a person's eyes. Had gone out. To hypnotize. I stayed awake. Weak in the knees am I. Not a spiritual woman. And pulled toward the earth.

▲

He said, you have to look from afar: what children we are, so gravely at play. In worn out light, in afterglow. Yet fire present is in words.

▲

Which is why we try to read. The stone, the wood and grass, the cloud and lightning and air. And the ancients and poets. And the frogs croak in the swamps.

▲

And to stand. Sky around your shoulders high on a mountain. Or balcony. And know you must cast. Like so many shadows. Your words onto the distance. Or paper. But will they span?

▲

And the next morning you go to the bakery and ask for a loaf of rye. This too is work and without it the dream crumbles inside its glass case. And we must travel the ocean just to see it.

4

With great force our bodies are pulled out of our mothers. And ever since, we walk like almost orphans. With a scar on the brain.

▲

And remember childhood among strings and puppets. Crutches. Knees under the chin tucked. And toy warriors with lance and shield and red badge to ensure courage.

▲

Which we need to live in three dimensions. Of dry air. Or wet. Among gauges for measurement made of wire and string. That my father had looked at before.

▲

And tapped with his finger to make sure. They were steady, not broken. And hitched his pants against gravity and tried to discern. The tether between particle and wave.

▲

Tea has dribbled on his book. The letters under the drops enlarge till a wavy gray absorbs the excess. If however too deep you plunge, he thinks. Into thought. You can't rest till you get to the bottom.

5

Let us take our time, Sophie, fitting bones to the earth.
Though they are turning visible inside the flesh, and our
blood. No longer overflows and spills.

▲

Much work still to be done. And the smell of ripe peach-
es. And Long-Jing tea. And lungs full of words. And being
an opaque body that intercepts the rays of the sun.

IV. UNACCOUNTABLE LAPSES

1

What is memory? A palace? The belly of the mind? Of absence a dream? The baby in the picture I don't remember, but I remember my doll.

▲

Knowledge with a flavor of thin air. The more invisible the fabric befits neighboring particles. But the sun's eaten in the sky and still. Its own body keeps. And where it is we pursue. So more like a piece of property to which I lay claim. Than a state of mind. Or androgyny. Or love of black pepper.

▲

In dark ivy I sat. In the shade of an oak. Just as noon poured down and lost wax. In my ears loitered. According to tradition. A shadow fell across clear-cut narration as I followed Wittgenstein to places. Where nothing happens.

▲

Even as I let wander my thoughts. The way blood cells cir-
culate to any part of the body. Or birds keep hopping.
From branch to branch. Which makes them hard to keep
track of. Unless I have words that don't fall. Between the
tracks.

▲

How many times can one single heart beat? So many
breaths deep and shallow. While the years pass without
hard edges. So I could put them end to end.

2

Animals do not hunt for a story. But blind am I in my soul. A fault is embedded. And were it not for the doll I would not. Know who I am. A pocket in space expanding less rapidly.

▲

A riddle is anything pure. In pure memory (what is pure memory? and where?) I might know my image. But not find a caption. Though a name of my own I have no matter what time of year.

▲

So should I inward turn? Breath held long enough to show. The rim of vertical time. Molecules into slower vibrations betrayed. A flake of death off the skin.

▲

Do we remain as we begin? Not to words then would thinking turn but to our first soaking sunlight. To rage raw and desperate cleaving the body. Like lightning the earth.

▲

So where must I search for my childhood? Among folds of the brain at the risk of falling between? Or in my throat an acid reflux? In order to repeat? What to complete I have failed? Until there's a hole in the window where I meant to toss the stone?

3

Maybe the past is enough for the past and all its inhabitants. They need not be drawn out of retirement. But if I repeat without knowing I repeat? Am I in my own body?

▲

Or is the past, like the Gods, without emotion? and gropes for our feelings lest it transparent turn? Like a woman not looked at? Fading between the pages of Grimm's *Kinder- und Haus-Märchen?*

▲

Meanwhile breath by breath down burns the house and under its rubble buries us. And great bodies of thought melt away. And no form identical to them ever again on the face of the earth appears.

▲

Though of love and sweet of summer traces float through arteries like great ships. Carrying kits for survival since the body is practical. And only when the brain's defenses are down, as in dreams, do we drown in the pure stream.

▲

The way Madame Blavatsky dipped her body in the Ganges and, says Yoel Hoffmann, said a prayer for plants. And did not consider the history of the earth and its reigns of silence and long sleep.

4

Not every fish has a jaw and many are the soft-bodied beasts our ancestors. And many forgotten beyond the shale of recall. Though their history can be read, some claim, in the cells of our body. The way language contains the layers of its development.

▲

And Dante said angels have no need of memory for they have continuous understanding. But we. To enter into thought. Need a bridge.

▲

But a mind obsessively drawn toward memory. Its own obstacle becomes. Like magnets pushed apart by the field they create. Or I enter the picture as a shadow because dumbly I get in the way of the light. And because I am shadow I cannot see.

▲

Or the way we cut open. Heads and x-ray our chests. In the effort to find love.

▲

Clustered on the tip of my tongue. Are names of species. Intermediate links that heard with their skin. Now missing for lack of. Or other reasons. While we improbable and fragile too. Head toward extinction.

▲

Not hard-shell certain the outcome in the match. Of recaller and recalled. And may alter both beyond recognition. Property is not passive.

5

Sudden the song of the blackbird and touches buried desire. You are there in the sound. What goes on in the soul that we must understand and can't?

▲

If the eye were a living creature, says Aristotle, its soul would be its ability to see.

▲

Skin stretches below the subconscious. The song gathers. In their straying flight. Lines that carry the weight of absence.

▲

This is a thirst that resembles me.

V. AT THE SEA

1   .

Down to the shore. And smell of brine. Away from moss, fern, mortar, brick. Form is fatal, some say. Whereas an endless unborn surface. Without point. Of reference. Containment. Or even vanishing.

▲

Here where the light is. Less hidden? Less dispersed into less things? Rolls in. White-crested. Splendor after splendor. Wall piled on wall. High as a house. And down comes crashing. Rocks. Severed heads. Centuries. And from the sand a thin veil of white recedes. And ripples and shadows and a ledge of clouds lined orange.

▲

Seeing is believing. But unthreatened by the dark are words. And there take refuge. Unshadowed. And thinking too takes refuge and then its own seed of light tries to sow.

▲

Pounding pounding the waves. Breath skyward drawn. Out of observable space, of muscular intuition. And the light goes on pretending that seeing is simple. That with mine own eyes have I touched. The shell in the sand. The fin of the minnow.

▲

I know the creed of light. We see. On condition of not seeing. The light. Transparent we dream the immediate.

2

With such amazing speed the eye. Of Ted Williams, say. Makes contact with the ball. It does not seem tied to its body. Does this reveal the nature of vision?

▲

Out at the sea I stare. As if it were the universe. Could pull the infinite into my eye. Without the rational lines of perspective. With absent wavelengths represented as imagination. Slow the eye I brought with me from Germany. And does not leave its body. Nor change the stance of distance.

▲

Blue. Two kinds of. Gray. Immersion. Open. Foam. Hallucination?

▲

Not toward. Not where I came from. No home beyond hard the sky limit. Away then? Seeing is leaving? The Western profile? The country whose mechanisms I understand no better than the light? And which. Like the light. Pretend they're not there.

▲

We come to a limit and stop. If there is no limit we cannot distinguish. Lost and no longer. I and everything else.

▲

Eyes breathe. Like open wounds.

3

Monet writes a friend he's painting "the instant." Succession stopped at success. A light his palette gives off. And color subdivided into into. On the retinal surface. Ground so fine. In each ray of light. Move motes of dust.

▲

Vibrations. Speed. Weather. Whatever blue.

▲

The killifish slip out of sight. Out of my mind: Sunrise. Tequila. "Ännchen von Tarau." Nails growing. Axons and dendrites. The dentist. My mother's maiden name. The ordinary physical scale.

▲

And how to talk to. I don't know. The dead. We've drained
the symbols so our stories be cool. But it would take. The
depth of years we stand on. The sea. Frequencies out of
range. And air. Insurmountable its lack of resistance.

▲

Which I breathe in and breathe out. And commit my
tongue to mate with the nick of time. And like a dream
bone worry it. And the sound of the words has no measur-
able size.

▲

Eyes wide open. Retinal warp. Into the distance where it
stops. Being distance. The brain turns pale and like to
freezing. The body takes a long time to reassemble itself.

4

Out of the word came the light. On the first day of cre-
ation. Introduced separation. From the dark. And time. In
alternation.

▲

The light took time. In its headlong flight. And knotted it
into space. Where we pursue happiness, always belated.
But the light did not remain. Unknotting the dimensions
back it went. Into the word. And time's left with nothing.

▲

Or the light neither returned nor issued. And needs no jus-
tification. But in the swells there's memory. Between crest
and trough. Of great upheavals.

▲

Refracts words. The light. Into runaway decay, instant loss. We make do with coins. And wish for slower language. Of darkness an eyeful. More local colors.

▲

Eyes cross the frontiers of glass. Penetrating. Penetrated. Like lovers. And like lovers rocked loose from the ground. By the grammar of convergence or some other force. Bloodstream pulled out to sea.

▲

Before slowed circulation and red sleep.

5

High tide. High above my head the water level. Rising. And thoughts float on it. Out of my depth. Their number displacing their weight. Movement in all directions, not going anywhere. A desk on the Atlantic.

▲

Eye without lid. Absorptive like a sponge of undecided sex. But I'm not made for all worlds.

▲

The light falls. On. Like the eye. And lingers. While its unseen colors try to penetrate under. The skin, for instance. And are blocked by the opaqueness of the body.

▲

Inward the nails grow later and the mind turns on itself. Myopic poison. And great ships sail over dry land.

▲

There is no clemency in the light. Or in the dark.

AS WERE

FOR STEVE EVANS

LEONARDO AS ANATOMIST, REPEATEDLY

To raise the ribs to dilate the chest to expand the lung to indraw the air to enter the mouth to enter the lung.

He plays on a tendon, decentered, opening the lungs of his name. Deluge. Unmoved by muscle, by act of will or without. By raising hopes in a calm and elegant direction.

In the evening, fleshy excrescence dilates a point on the lower lip where it flowers in an unmistakable "no" displacing breath.

Fat extends the fin-de-siècle from dinner to dinner. Witness the joint. Of the bone to which this dotted line is attached.

What if smiling expands the chest westward? Or property is threatened as an organ touches visibility, as there is no vacuum, as a pair of bellows?

To thicken the space with reverberations rather than imprint the sinewy force of pigment. To spur a feminine ending.

Rings under his eyes, clairvoyant. Otherwise unlit.

To raise the ribs to dilate the chest to expand the lung to indraw the air to enter the mouth to enter the lung.

VESALIUS AS APPRENTICE, FABRICATION

FOR MARY CAPONEGRO

Clearly on the dissecting table the reason for parts and position acquainted entire the fabric of nature

The apprentice with a syringe with skin to peel with no thought of the old man he will be

Candle fed by the fat of life

Clearly the number position and shape and no doubt contradiction very clearly

Patently the apprentice with his syringe given the finger with no thought of ill of infirm of the chamberpot he might need by his bed

Wrongly remembered becomes murky smoke

Then the function of muscles imagine through glass where thickens acquainted entire pockets permitting a limb

Tourniquets did little to stay the

The apprentice with his syringe with light bright as advertising with no thought of his funeral of who might weep who send flowers

Death extends as far as the smoke continues

Hand in pocket hardly one for dissecting the living clearly the contradictions are many

MONTAIGNE AS MAYOR,
IN MOTION

———————————

Never in our selves, but beyond. The best stoics are bred
by displacement. No other stern old men in nightshirts
matter. Although the account of the journey is structured
on water rising above the axiom level he closes the shutters
against bad weather. Pronounce: theology. The pain of a
kidney stone is fierce. There is a continual need for
women in labor.

Study can draw the soul and quarter it outside the body.
Though startled by riots over a tax on salt. Collected
together on shelves, the best stories breed islands or blan-
kets of gray matter. Severe nausea in combination with the
feeling that his spine lies broken on a gurney. Once he
knows that the incomprehensible is incomprehensible he
makes careful note of the fact. Voracious attention feathers
into collateral branching on the way to the thalamus.
Confused by the boldness of women.

Speculative manner on a wine-growing estate outside
Bordeaux creates its own glass darkly. For if the world were
only what it is, would it be the case? Scrutinizes his urine in
the chamber pot. The temperature of a body of philosophy.

———————————

Acts on many cells at once, like lightning. His is a time when the body is part of the personality. So the joke is against him.

Exchanges public life for uncertainty, reflection, apprenticeship of death. Reads everything, quotes everybody, but does not look in the mirror held up by woman. We Bordelais. Urine full of painful gravel. Without embarrassment, the animal body. Objectivity, a wish fulfilled only in dreams. Soon after, the kidney disappears from literature.

HERNANDO DE SOTO AS WRITER, INTREPID

Sailed from Havana, cast seven days' anchor, discovered the Mississippi—to the surprise of the red men not in a rush to become deckhands. The writer at her desk begins with a convulsion of the thumb and index finger or, sometimes, the big toe. She wants his body. To change geometry just as space curves near a large mass.

Talks too much, book on the floor, spine torn, vain, boastful, sand in her mouth, drinks ink, beside herself with

Reasonably certain he looked across the river, maybe stopped swearing, but did he look at the muddy current, how it rushes and overspreads the swamps? As the writer's doubts sooner or later spread across her fleet of nine vessels. We avoid these spasms by holding on to definitions of the rigid body and three meals a day.

Sudden calamity, carried off, the current, eddies, rafts, ridges, too clotted for narrative, rings under her eyes, too slow for a long life

His gaze, like most men's, on the far side of the evolutionary process, with hardware confidence. But the writer, "exceeding ready" with her words when there's already much bad grammar. And what should we interpret as physical deformation of a body, what as geometry of space?

Sandbanks, swollen waters, foam, crevasse in the levee, plastic bags, needles, telephone numbers, one silver spoon, not in her mouth

Remained to die and be buried beneath its waters, so his pact with the river not superficial. Is it worth while to pile on turbid water invention, hallucination, déjà vu, and a horror of death? And what is a force—I mean something to change a body?

Gators, damn it, oaths as detonating commas, sold down the river, fuck, with the lights on, cacolalia, phrases filched from

GOETHE AS TYPE, MORPHOLOGICAL

The parts of matter, their respective form, their relations, their special character.

Mass of heart, part sediment, part scatter. Within, algorithms metabolize their own labor and heat. Which is to say, darts and tickles toward the woman in red.

The form of minerals unmoved. Quick, a horse. Resist showdown to the ocean bed ridden with afterlife, forgotten derivations.

He claims his name with moist inflection and hands. Both structure and outer shape decidedly freeway complexity. Jarring seeds, atoms shattered. Birth of subterranean heft.

He runs toward wavelength, stochastic variables, and sometimes west. The color of declination, of character. And how porphyry shines out of the post-partum mountain like simplicity.

Whereas the inter- and overleaved double crystals in Karlsbad granite cannot stop infinite regress. Smaller facets swim close to tears.

Igneous, plutonic, some metamorphic. Fact and its strong, gusty wind. Neuronal norms, with much longing. Also apply to beautiful gardener. What does whose body want?

A storm of undecidability, unfit for market or military purposes. We might imagine two interlaced rhomboid planes and lay bare a fist on the table, a fleeing widow and child.

MALLARMÉ AS PHILOLOGIST, DYING

FOR MARJORIE WELISH

Even the purest writer is not entirely in his work, we must admit. A saturated white tilts off the page, a ricochet of sense like children heard, not understood. You see the gap between chance breath and the continuous line of the horizon, method to infinite power or out one candle. Anatole *aboli*. *Bibelot* Anatole. Walks down the stairs, one by one, to the bottom of the mirror. It is the lack of self splits his ear. A labyrinth like a sentence. Always, word follows word, to stave off those little deaths. Is he alive?

When he leaves the room, he recaptures a memory called meaning. A matrix where a word is carried by a foreign language. Say "th." Say the whole word: "death." The *Box for Learning English by Yourself and Playing* is broken, the string to push the puppet's tongue between his teeth. "Debt" is not comparable, not part of the body. Throw the dice, throw. Again. If often enough, only everything. Between the teeth.

To track your dream, enter by way of the corridor and comparative grammar. The dream is called work. The corridor leads to Hebrew, which shows how to replace lacking inflection by ideal nakedness. The corridor passes time, so that the girl is cold. When you caress her name, somber and red like an open pomegranate, you slowly descend toward. Stop. The dream insists that meaning, memory, and music are the same. Out of its own lack, it fashions a flesh of vowels, and of consonants a skeleton delicate to dissect. What is a faun to do?

A simple laryngitis. Does not abolish breath. A lacking word, a thought that terrible would vibrate suffocating like an open spasm splits his ear terrible his throat. Geneviève, virgin spasm, vivacious, and beautiful today suffocating. A fan of lacking experiences. For Mademoiselle Mallarmé. It is hot. Wants a book on anatomy, it cannot be too simple: he might place the larynx in the brain. Again. His breath stops, and we are all speechless.

TATLIN AS TOWER, ERECT

He confuses an interest in curved paths. Open snow light. Curve after curve across material and constructive relations. If you kiss a woman rising from her chair you may fall over your feet. He confuses "if I kissed" with curve by definition.

Looking from above, in the thin light. She clearly discerns two spirals rising around a cause which is the effect of its effect. She has to hold on. The spirals rise like snow. She falls into error or asleep.

The original idea supported by curved girders. Curled in reverse, uncautious, many wooden laths. Held in the air inside his mind like birds. The light like a knife, and gives a little twist. We're out of love intrigues.

Against the artist's intention there emerges an outer and an inner space. She spirals down between them. Like the umbilical cord, the light. At the rate of one revolution per kiss. Slowly, up to the waist in snow, her consciousness returns inside her skin.

The curvature corresponds to wings. The slowest most concave. Light falls inside the snow, reflecting gravity. He has to look at his feet to keep his balance. The different parts of the wing do not have the same speed.

Gliding was enormously popular in the twenties. Birdlike craft on bicycle wheels, rising, with eyes and beak like a figurehead. Photographs at regular intervals in Soviet publications. She turns to feel her skin taut in the cold. She does not fall.

The more curious machines in time. The tower during erection. It is repetition makes the scaffolding and makes it fall. The spiral's curve can be computed as eternal return. It does not explain how to stay upright.

KAFKA AS SON, IRREVOCABLY

He always thought it best he smelled ashamed in what is called a body, but business is bad. Less daily interval than hat raised to strange goings-on. Without visible means.

No tales here in the office, no soap, no samples. What is this light, as if an emanation, falls and onto what?

Common sense or silence. Compare ticklish.

Material world specific the. Unmoved while the audacious soul backstrokes against its current. From which a flock of doves and colored ribbons.

Lemons. Bellies. Such misfortunes. [belly dance here] Be unsteady. Your not already state. Flings grain outside the mother tongue.

Of hand on shoulder. Of father climbing in bed with the son. Fallen light then falling right again. Impossible. Impass.

One must distinguish.

Between last night and hesitating to be born.

Accordingly in doubt. In exile among explanations. "In" "stinct." The son being devoured. Had requested and all manner of siren.

Here he allowed himself. As he was. Though not sleeping.

Unease. Unfinished wall. Sliding obstacles.

He didn't know if. Cheeks flushed with visitors. Foot dangling. Or why he was no longer young. Wearing a fur coat a few minutes before solitude. Then carried back to the closed door.

STEIN AS EXACT
RESEMBLANCE, EXACT

Strangely simultaneous the larger the crowd at work. Strangely identical phenomena the more distant yellow splashed. Chatter angelic gesture polite honey so beguiling strangely.

Did spend time to be meant among opaque could save the sentence. Did spend into the world once an angry man is no wiser a sentence. Goes on elsewhere dragged we think along the ground did spend.

When we listen astounding no longer listen the midst of bewailing. When we listen a temporary umbrella a candle a quart of sleep. Of swept water flushed out of sound out of sound when we.

Plenty of space plenty of ordinary plenty of present. With plenty of dust to cover a single event and no comma it's nothing. Means nothing in spite of assembles assembles plenty.

His body is the distance that separates him from his object.
A definition must precede measurement and reminis-
cences. Everyday actions, like she came down the stairs,
multiplied by population. More than heroic energy. A slap
in the face, a bite from a dog, a pair of coordinates, fic-
tional lucky numbers.

His strange attachment to the visible even when there is
no fountain. Mistake: to think the definitions cannot
change. A piece of paper. Without anything written on it.
She pauses, trying to remember all that might just as well
be different.

He is one with the distance that separates him from his
body. There is no logical objection to this. Possibility not
only includes a sudden toothache, but the yet unawakened
intentions of gods. Which divide the body impartially.
Breath, flickering side effects, energy from the inside.

Every sensation sides with the world. In practice, a breeze
through the brain. A possible experience does not equal
real experience minus the value of real. Nor a woman who

mails parcels to her children. Fingers feeling right under the skin.

He tries to distance himself from distance. In this connection "small area" means "on the order of the size of the earth." A possible experience, according to its followers, is something divine, a will to structure, fire, flight in quick succession. But she is dead. Separate out familiar and simultaneous.

His strange attachments. No logical objection can be advanced in small areas. So that philosophers could see what kind of unborn forest for the trees. He takes refuge in the next thing to be done. He'd go mad inside the blindspot, the place of no proof.

An A to follow, following form. Say A. Innocent object. Pregnant and. Sawhorses. Lack heads and necks. What?

▲

Musicians underpaid. With an accent. For forty-six years. Counter Troy? Point Gethsemane? Cobbled?

Replace inward the ground for dance, replace deepest.

A fullness above the lute. A fiction. All and more sleepless in a city.

Least Latin music matched to English evening. Most surface. Arpeggio maned to private weather. Parts by heart.

Follows talk about graves.

▲

Spare. Bit cold. Knots among stridencies. As music washed back to limit. Upper. Than.

The Brooklyn Bridge with childhood in tow.

Letters by heart. Unstowed. Grow birds. Child of burned sleep. The alphabet knits uncurved proof.

Let the audience look to their eyes. Of deep but helplessly naked.

Flows love. In itself. To reason.

BLINDSIGHT

"THE I UNDOES THE FIELD"

—JOHN KINSELLA

ACQUIRE WITHIN

Want of space prevents me, however sharp the winter in Rhode Island. We distinguish between central, or direct, and peripheral vision. Between constant and vapor, picture and whirl. Leaves and fishes. Intimacy at degree 0. A protracted childhood, a girl for good. No sudden deviation, no wheeling flock of birds.

Fear of man is slowly acquired. Did not marry and so lived on in her father's house. A stiff chair beside the bed, a candlestick, an illustrated Bible. Bone button conduit. Weak from vapors. There is considerable interest in the problems of space perception, of shadows falling outside the fovea. Winter moved slowly.

Even in New England, the large birds are wilder than the small, having been most persecuted. The door from her room led into another childhood. All space locked. Instead of historical background, relatives appeared at the window, at eye level. Loaves and dishes. Every retinal point stimulated emits unconscious local signals. The periphery was always hers.

Whereas on uninhabited islands, large birds are not more fearful than the small. She stared vacantly into spaces between floorboards. Eyes swimming, looking for land. The finger is moved from various parts of the periphery inward. On the bright rectangle of the blind, the shadow of the pear tree. A heterogeneous assortment of signals, with a view to illustration, the core of intimacy not specific as to location.

Audubon has noted remarkable differences in nests of the same species. She settled in the space inside her name. It is a peculiarity that a locked door recaptures early loves and wishes. Only by describing the relation between purpose and picture can she sever her father from her body. This assumes that every peripheral point has a capacity for being central, but deception is more frequent.

URGENT SILT

I will not attempt to deflower instinct. We'd have to crack the code, cultivate systems of hair. The old man owned three women by marriage, birth, or contract. Only one dream survives, hanging upside down. The parts immediately surrounding the eye must also receive attention. Imagine, if you can, the no man's land the water surrenders and reclaims.

Everyone understands that instinct impels the cuckoo to lay her chill on other birds' nests. Narrow as the coffins the old man had made his forethought. The riddle of the dream doesn't have to be solved, but systematic examination may be divided into a) objective, b) piercing instruments. By the shore, sand under eyelids. Think how wet a sob long repressed.

Under changed conditions, however, it is at least possible that modifications survive the code. Tense in his armchair, trying to ignore the cracks in the floor. Few of his social class patted swollen bellies in order to get to know Darwin. Sun. Wheel. Eye behind the eye. A dream the color of sand absorbs excess water.

No instinct being known amongst extinct species, the arm-chair is not used. The old man was ready to weep with vexation. Examination by means of palpation and binocular parallax is conducted in the sweaty month of August, revealing a long face. The seaboard followed the swollen eye. Many burrowed into the damp daylight.

Indispensable for the action of natural selection, heat gathers. How often an insight is accompanied by dreams of prey. We commence with the lids, noting their thickness, color, and position. When light begins to show through the crack of dawn, the loud crashing of the waves subsides.

PROFIT

Any one of a number of unknown causes. These woods in your stead, this weathered circumstance. Astonished he dreamed perfect blackness. Although "aging" merely means growing older the word is seldom used without the bodily faculties playing chicken. The brain has its muscles, but whom do they obey?

Could the organism then suffice? For shipwreck in private parts? He stood inside his mouth. It is in reality a natural process bringing on weather, cars screeching, angles of sight detached from the eye. Beginning with brute matter. With strontium's sinister quest for bones.

All animal flesh palpitates after death. These woods in your head. In spite of a purchase on triceps tightening, heat, and lust, aging begins at birth. The growth rate cut loose at a loud sixteen, falling. Maybe you don't mind being deceived.

The brain of a piece with storms, wisdom with teeth. Likewise graying hair not accompanied by increase in gray matter or acid rain. He hoped she would be maternal, but she floated undisturbed by wet clothes. Religion might happen next.

Each tiny fiber purchases its role. The wood in your bed. Looking for what's lost. The very bulk of the human heart, only smothered. Menopause is a sign that one class of hazard has been outlived. Instead, sky teeming with lions, loaves and fishes, unicorns.

Is it by mechanical means that the pores close in autumn? These woods in red. Without comfort of violins. There is no known reason why aging would have to be mudslides, pale winter syntax, brakes and no stepping on them. We have trouble imagining patterns of thought which exclude profit.

LATENT SETTLEMENT

At length we abandoned the Cartesian method for the whalebone corset, which squeezes the viscera toward the absent lover. When the Cherokee Sequoyah tried to create a written language for his tribe he took a deep breath away from his lungs. The temperature dropped in the midst of religious struggles. Instead of foreplay he believed in the sun.

We will term the cause latent in the pulp of the nerves (and not as yet ascertained) the *vis nervosa*. She wore a heavy linen napkin strapped between her legs in blanket anticipation. This is almost equivalent to saying that a dementing heat was projected upon her "envelope." Having broken the words down into syllables, Sequoyah buttoned his clothes.

External impressions are very quickly transmitted along the whole length of the nerve. No woman at the end of her tether, especially when standing, would rely on the other hand. A match. A flatiron. The history of seduction not to be dissociated from the vessels in which it was transported, the cups from which it was drunk. Sequoyah borrowed letters from the English and touched the recipients.

As the spark is latent in steel or flint, and not elicited unless there be friction, out of sorts as she is, she will menstruate. For contained and container form, in fact, a single critique of reference. Amid other traffic, 86 characters in search of a Cherokee author to enter their parts. Of speech. They did not hold the sun accountable for the consequences.

This is not performed according to mere physical laws, to mercury in giddy ascent. Wearing all these clothes as proof of privacy, she must go down to the cellar woodpile, too poor to afford language. In 1821 appeared the first bilingual newspaper, the CHEROKEE PHOENIX, and in 1840 the image on the retina was inverted. It is perfectly natural for the sun to shine in the upper left-hand corner of this page.

THIS

When the medulla oblongata is pricked, or in any other way irritated, white furious sun high in a state of tension. Shed her clothes and inexplicably married. Caught in the fact. Solitary muscles, such as the sphincter, are always contracted. The first representations of Amerindians showed naked men and women gnawing on a human leg with equal opportunity. Her husband avoided looking directly into her face.

While nervous power is necessary to muscular motion the sun cannot be replaced by logic. Hence the inhabitants of New England have never made friends without blinds drawn. He pulled his pants up. The Indians stood between quotation marks. While an oblique ray of sunlight penetrates a silk blouse the stimulus is shown as consistent. In all his life, he had seen nothing that so attacked his heart.

Likewise, a quick thrust on the toe pad excites a shade too sure of herself. Subcutaneous itch. To fight it out in whispers, in degrees Fahrenheit. Desire flaked off the shoulder of the highway, by way of blaming the sun. To introduce difference into the all-or-nothing theory, the women wore no covering other than a narrow cloth over their privates.

A heavy penetrating odor caught on the person of her husband.

The sun's influence on nerves, even in small quantities, seals them in paraphrase. As nature intended. There was hair on the rest of his body. In the upper half of the picture, the condition of sight itself. The longer the Indians stood in the sun, the more it turned their eyes back into their body. This is how she knew she was pregnant.

INSTEAD OF SPLINTERS

The fingers of the young child bend around every itch on the palm well before the factory whistle clocks it in. While the perceived magnitude of a star is a function of its brilliance, we may still wipe our eyes with the corner of a handkerchief. How shy she was of herself. Copperplate engravings of American flora appeared at the end of the sixteenth century and prompted rites of passage to the New World.

That desire precedes any showing of hands can be explained in most latitudes: such is the power of language. The girl survived though her body was naked. Passing from the center to the periphery of the retina we expect to find a tunnel or prepaid equivalent. Copper offers a precision of line superior to souvenirs or flotsam.

We must distinguish the automatic from the voluntary to which the city owes its eminence in the cotton trade. But a hand not taken in marriage? Nor the textile mills? Nobody could call the New England summer lovable. The girl had a peculiar way of handling things, so hesitant, hard to map, yet able to reproduce flowers on frocks.

When points on the retina are intense enough to light a cigarette there is nothing to be grasped. How long a word before it slides through our fingers? Off the assembly line? The girl simply disappeared from the neighborhood. Though very few pictures of America had circulated before the light turned red.

Let the reader judge if it was heat or humidity that made furthermore intolerable. Bad news due to defects of the eye as an optical instrument. Better to map the motions of the body with sentences at least equally strange. When the girl returned, most of the population did not even suspect another continent on the make.

At last, that state of mind we call the will to grasp clings like a low fever and cannot be shaken off. Its diameter increases with pleasure promising difficult respiration. How can I help myself, she said, empty as a pronoun, as the baby's puny fists pumped up and down.

CERTAINTIES

A frame supports what would, on its own, collapse. Apple trees pilfered from a novel, the firmest possible squeeze of the hand. The same skin in and out. But we can laugh to dissolve the already. Though there are things that elude us, there for the money.

Perception surprisingly accurate. The sky seemed forever. The only defense against exaggerated sounds is to stop your fears. We're moving toward a global situation. Not in anyone's shoes. In weather. History upon us like mother. But laughter equals disobedience. How fragile things, how thin the cortex.

This fact led to the belief that the "properties" of objects are conducted by nerves to the mind. We forthwith invested in solid brick and mortar. In unmitigated promises. Laughter, like other interruptions of breath. Accidental sex. Not self-contained like music. There is always someone coming in from the street unfreezing the frame, cutting across the certainties of eye.

One needs to distinguish. Just as thrift has a different meaning for the poor. His back obsolete against the wall. Squeezed, with a strange desire to accumulate apples. The dynamics of a single sound. Only consonants should be used to brush against information.

The entire visual field is excited. But skin sticks to the bones with parsimony. Likewise, our dreams have been compacted into a single coin. Of reasonable size. A buttoned frame of mind suggested by the neck. He locked up the trees. In the middle distance, a laugh shakes us out of focus.

By contrast, our conscious skin is patchy. Therefore we sleep fully dressed. Once we let go of the frame, a sudden interest in the body. Given the uncertain status of the real, laughter a sudden glory. An apple tree gets repeated, and it is music.

LENS

Our capacity for learning is closely concerned with memories of milking cows. Nothing repeats itself except history. The palace, in winter. Now that long sentences are in disuse, blood is not diverted into causes. Nor does the gesture of shivering produce the sensation of labor pains. The first picture of a person wearing spectacles is in a fresco of 1352.

The rate of learning new words does not affect a child's central nervous system, but modifies history. And Gothic Revival for American farm houses. Is it by accident that Bechterev lectured on reflex in 1917? Meta-mathematics might well unveil meta-dimensions and, with the right equation, loss of an entire world. The fresco is by Tommaso Barisino di Modena. The impulse to speak somehow annulled.

When rays impinge on the ends of the optic nerve, they open onto revolutionary metaphors. The farmer intrepid. The feeling abridged. The words "it makes me shiver" are themselves compacted windshields. Skin boasting the latest nudity. Rafters of light timber that require neither deep foundation nor complete skylines.

When the infant learns her first word she has been listening to both her mother. The laboratory Pavlov dreamed of was absolutely soundproof. Though a cry is not a description, we must adhere to analogy with nature. The center for lens grinding from which eyeglasses were diffused to the rest of civilization was Holland. A narrative, however, in which blood flows is more likely to develop an only child.

We harvest Dutch elm disease and retinal warp. Cows, in pasture. It was the same part of Holland from which the style of Tommaso's painting derives. After a flood in the laboratory, the dogs forgot all conditioned reflexes. Just as a child of bilingual parents and a child in the orphanage draw separate lines to the past. Which will not be told again.

MENSURATIONS OF
THE MOON

———————

Of all the lovers emphatically erect. And incomprehension, of which there's always more. The word animal not mentioned in the Bible (though many beasts). Then stirred the coffee, the depth of years, the optic nerve. A schedule of changing pleasure, approximate seasons, now cooled now culled. How large her eyes. Whenever she cannot sleep.

From astonished to abashed. A flaw between bed and absent-minded. Her face was difficult to look at. Less than a month after construction, the world. Cattle and every creeping thing. A body of water too can make love. And live with us hereafter.

Then let us consider how bodies operate one upon another. How rational construction is worn thin by expressways. How silence falls with the leaves. A girl raised in the Northeast, imagination striped with muscle. The relation of mind and mushroom, beauty and beast. A little sweaty.

Look don't touch. Though curiosity lengthens her body. A jaw so jutting, so extreme. Affection welled up from the diaphragm. Next to it, in the shadow, she laid a piece of white paper of the same bigness. So that it became possible to dream of a more comprehensive later. Of looking out into the garden in the faint light of delusion.

Invisible currents between people. Killing animals does the rest. Tradition abrupt on individual talent. No matter how much she ate, she never got warm. The sound is repeated to experience the eclipse again. Just as eyes grow more luminous in fear.

Musical effects rare, unlike spiritual values. Three hundred species of animals have become extinct. Hearing the word snowball might well excite vigilance in the hollow of the year. But don't look more closely. You'll miss a breath, the double intensity when eyes meet. Yet it's not certain the early girl gets the word.

ANTIBODY

A sour home. Aroused by intrusion into the body. The manner and the fear no more than ankle deep. She feels stranded. The end of each muscle transformed into tendon. Objects, activities, emotions now will not hold together.

The fat white stepmother who loves modified blood protein. The portrait calmly waits for the model to die. As she puts on weight it extends toward impartial. She couldn't think of another word.

Has not budged an inch from understood to mean. The reaction between antibody and antigenic substance is exquisitely specific. She never dared the middle. Which successively. Sensations or perceptions drained from one person to another in conversation. We want our stories cold.

Coming events cast their shadow. Accepted as immunity in court. The blank hiatus between blood and guts. The evidence to which this muscle is attached. She would have refused new bones from the East.

Now the face haunts you, you look again and again. You hope for antibodies to enter the locked room. Put an eye to the lens, and it'll answer, though the word order may be wrong. These muscles have voluntary and involuntary minds. She hasn't said no. A glassy surface shorn of its fleshy parts.

Such solitude. So oblivious of the camera. The ability to form antibodies compressed by the contracting muscles. She does not remember who took the picture. Approaching chill prevents. As if suffering from breath.

IMAGES

A rash of perceptible things like in shape to solid bodies. Time snaps in two, and she sees herself. Submerged logs, shells of mollusks, the teeth of whales. The seat of the soul where all the senses meet is called common sense. The I undoes the field.

She is not herself today though the eye of God remains on the dollar. Images move with unsurpassable speed, worth a thousand words. Most barnacles are hermaphroditic, all atoms uniform. If we look at brightness with a magnifying glass we only see more brightness. The soul will respect no props.

Images form quickly because they need not be solid inside. She doesn't weep, this one, it isn't her nature. The lights go out. Silence as one might see in a lake. Nerves, tendons, common sense. No exchange takes place outside the mother tongue and queasy stomach.

Objects could not make an impression by means of air, but images are cunning. A sudden downpour this side of idolatry. Fish, birds, a friend by mistake. Darwin came to have doubts. As soon as the image has a name, it haunts you. How sense waits on soul, and soul on sense, is called the origin of language.

The faculty of vision goes out from the brain to meet the image in the optic nerve. If she sets herself against a background into which she cannot merge her face flushes a mottled red. Light does not pass through, but falls upon. Nevertheless the nerves sometimes work by themselves, skipping bargains with strange gods.

When an image enters us day trembles on the brink and we are almost young. The sun no more shows all its colors than heat is a definition of seduction. She adapts too quickly. So that the barnacles are sure to win. The word soul is immortal, but the picture is painted on an uncurved surface. This is how it takes us in.

CORNELL BOXES

ENIGMA BOX

Am I caught in the stare of a Medici prince or do I hold him in the cross hairs?[1] I myself have always been quietly alert. In my dream I both stood at the stern and struggled under water, but a gun is another story. Don't step on the shards, she cries, not with bare feet, so frightening the smart missiles, the limits of time and space, the implicational character of mathematical demonstration.

Marbles, cordial glasses, soap bubbles reflect the sensual world, while around my navel there is concentrated a circular[2] red rash. I am extremely interested in failure. The beginning of art lies next to the body, transitive fissure, with high waves immediately behind. Sun, sea, severance, and people in the street, she cries, what deviance from curved diameter and straightest line.

The intimate scale of childhood also attracts hourglass, clay pipe, and intelligent collaborators. Others may prefer columns of a smaller diameter,[3] but a Mediterranean garden surrounds my Northern mind. I feel her tiny wet tongue licking my finger. The ocean, she cries, glare, wind, salt, scattered islands, limited income, it's not encounters in cabins, but chains of logical relations that compel proof.

Most remarkable, the presence of the egg. In a sea so calm not the slightest tremor suggested the tides of sexual impulse threatening the individual. The fact that we dream night after night surpasses the most heated fantasies. What lavish, wasteful refraction of light, she cries, deserted planets, desperate obsessions, do I have to invent everything all over, and without auxiliary concepts like the curvature[4] of a surface?

1 to define with accuracy, a story on shards

2 perfect, *obs.*, unease

3 through the center, and you must feed

4 the invisible if it exists across my eye

ICE BOX

He is fascinated by the parallel seams in the ship's sails, the threads of the web. But I am not some kind of psychic casualty, I simply want to please.[1] You know, in the winter of 1835, in Russia, Marie Taglioni's carriage was halted by a highwayman? A barely perceptible, she sighs, an uncertain, and how he approached with bare feet along a line of perspective without being able to, without touching—and yet we stay on the surface and do not measure the *real diameter* through the inner parts.

If he dreams of a wooden ball with a long needle sticking through it no one in America knows more coldly accurate. The whiteness of the ship is everywhere, a short-time slice against tidal connotations. The enchanting creature was commanded to dance for this audience of one upon a panther's skin spread over the snow. Intimate turn, the unmarried moon, she sighs, so foreign, stunned senses, I panic, take flight as if the third dimension alone could tell crooked from straight.

While fervently admiring healthier possibilities, I take my florid face out of the menu and feel my armpits growing dry. What is the relation between the large particles we

call elephants,[2] and the extremely small ones we call mol-
ecules[3] or fading passage? This is the counsel of despair,
snow between stars. And years later, she sighs, a disap-
pointed smile, our eyes for a, as if his double, the feeling
of it gone, and the ratio changed between circumference
and diameter.

He had a special star-shaped box made the more menac-
ing. I resented this and rearranged the napkin in my lap.
The motivation of biological mechanism[4] falls short of the
Puritan plan. Severely ship-shape she placed a piece of ice
among her jewels. First thought on waking, she sighs, dust
whirling in slant light, the excessive whispers, the flight of
time, but the curvature of space is the more flagrant struc-
ture.

1 the light of other days
2 elect: electrons, shimmering relation
3 feel deeply and a hint of atmosphere on sphere
4 atoms tropical, our fading passage

JACK IN THE BOX

IN MEMORY OF JOHN HAWKES

The enemies of the novel are plot, character, setting, and theme, you said, but the marquise still goes out at five, and at the stern where we were standing together but separated, it was impossible to hear the engines of the ship. The alternatives of free[1] will and causal determination do not exclude each other, though problems arise if we look for truth where definitions are needed. I heard the sudden hiss of urine. Fist through glass, you said, her legs straddling the railing, underclothes ravaged from an invisible clothesline, pollen, hollows of the body, such tension.

Everything is dangerous, you said, everything tentative, nothing certain, life jackets engulfed by crosscurrents, the thrashing of the great blades just below us and innocence in extremis. There would be contradiction only if a man could see through himself,[2] which is as impossible as knowing if a measuring rod retains its length when taken to another planet. Suppose instead we enter a period of midriffs, of second skins. Ja-Ja-Ja, you said quickly, the eye, bodily, the despotism of the uterine, odorous, earthen, vulval, convolvaceous, saline, mutable, seductive.

Can you rivet your eyes on the close-by,[3] we asked, and yet turn them toward hemispheric distances, can you crowd a spare sentence with absence and spare it? The question whether causality applies to actions of your own will is a travesty as pure and dark as a blackened negative. It's dreadful, dreadful no one has yet seen a wavelength. Of speech or suffocation, you said, white cadences, cold fire, hair like a dense furry tongue, natural lace, beetle leg, scar, a field of blood.

The enemy of pleasure, you said, is the curve of probability and flat exit. And so science must acknowledge singing in the wake of pubic darkness. A different geometry would obtain if we had rigid bodies. No turning back of time, you[4] said, unbearable sunlight, gunmetal ocean, Irish eye, glass splinters, a dream of flying and falling, a deep leap into, while the rest of us stand here, stabbed with sorrow.

1 Cf. fall, hold, lance, wheeling, dom, for all

2 and smoke five Dutch cigars

3 a single fly, buzzing

4 knife, daw, rabbit, straws, o'-lantern, in the pulpit, in the box

STAR BOX

Orion, the hunter, high over my head; the Dog Star follows him through the night even though his legend is different, monstrous, two-headed. Victorian dress no safeguard against excess or waning empire. Nor can we be sure the story accurately represents the underlying power lines. A single pigeon cooing on the roof, a phallus in the void, I didn't know, she whispers, what time of day, already dark, and if my feet went to his house all by themselves.

When history is emblematic,[1] the course of ruin can be put in reverse or the sky. A frantic innocence: a flock of doves: the virgin Pleiades. Though the abolishment of capitalism is not inevitable, fireflies next time. As if he couldn't understand, she whispers, heart in my throat, seafoam, feather on the floor, foot fetish, common sense skin, owl, or measuring eye.[2]

But the gridwork is fragile, the constellations a trick of perspective, the idea of sleep replaced by sleepiness. I prefer local intervals in ideology. And if not innocence, at least the taste of clear cold water as it comes from under the rocks. The encounter with Einstein never took place, she whispers, throat constricted, head tossed back toward the dark green feathered beauty, brought compass, sea salt, licorice, solar set, and the layered pink of the untitled palace, but forgot the question must be stated exhaustively.

This compulsion to connect the dots into story, meaning, and insomnia. The body says "I" all by itself, and history's a mishap in the statistics. Yet the obliteration of constellations by the same act that formed them is almost as radical a shock as the invention of "realism."[3] Complex, the relation between social fact and and after-sex beauty, she whispers, painful secret, unusual effect, the eye in the peacock feather wet with tears, is "real"[4] a meaningful concept?

1 with utmost nakedness
2 partition particles
3 the dial turns, the yellow painted sun has set, a single pigeon on the
     roof
4 no known address

LETTER BOX

FOR CLAUDE ROYET-JOURNOUD

To encounter anything fully is to touch its absence, but she could not possibly wish me to kiss her lips. There's something physical about the middle of a book, a *locus of hunger*.[1] Just as the passion for seeing survives on its own sweetness, defining reverses concepts to other concepts. "Transparency of nerve," he writes, "smallness of talk, a green unruffled marble, obsessed with contiguity, periphery of language, grammar of margins."

But the center is always dissolving, hole nailed through line, sentence, and the demon of analogy. The slightness of her body was brushing against all the bulk of mine. This coordination is not arbitrary and may be explained, like the erratic course of certain stars, by a *dark companion* with strong gravitational pull. "Mouth open to earth," he writes (but will it nourish?) "obsessed with deviation, hand caught in a page, the body to come, got no tongue, will fall, the crack opens, abrupt obstacle."[2]

Something to upset the balance: *a negative dungheap, a beast dismembered on the spot*. The smallest alteration in the world of physical objects, like this photograph placed on my suitcase, produces the severest and most frightening transformations of the infinite. Whereas in physical knowledge, concepts are coordinated with particular things in a testable relation.[3] "He starts small," he writes, "hunts for his tongue, daylight doggedly, takes the place of childhood, time at a loss, hitch in the language, leaves the boat, rushes into"

A different relation to knowing, the pursuit cannot define the object of pursuit even if the road is lit by a crystal cage, lighthouse, bright red plumage, high noon. I was not surprised to be alone.[4] Certain coordinative definitions must be determined before we measure the indivisible. "I understand something quite different," he writes, "moves forward in the dark, defines the margin, bulks large in what, as if nothing, to no one."

1 "cramped sun"
2 "the native speech of"
3 "he sees a spot coming closer to where he's waiting for it"
4 "cold reaches its target"

CINDER BOX

Virtuoso of fragments, master of absences.[1] Was she about to smile or replace the glass slipper with the notion of variables? No sharp line of demarcation[2] between organism and environment because blood in the shoe. Warning cry, raven, more in my head, lunar eclipse, she cries, not stored in the brain but spread throughout the body, rewind of nightmare to single out the actual kingdom among possible untitled.

The variable demands that we think both the stable and unstable, the invariant within the variation. Her lashes, like the physical sensation of the I. Do not assume the alogical core of the world is a pumpkin at midnight or stepmother. His look sharp like a camera, barely blinking, she cries, were there cinders in the cellar, were there mountains, other daughters, was it possible to measure the space in which we do not understand?

A spiraling watch spring, the fullness of time,[3] knots, neighborhoods, snug fit. He should not have revealed his loneliness, distaste for travel, ambiguous feeling toward women, or the intense activity within the atom on which its mass and other prophecies depend. Stop muttering in

Italian, she cries, images stored in my head, doors not properly balanced, it all always vanishes, as if to prove I have not looked, just taken pictures. With due respect to losses (slippers) we must return to the slot machine.

Is the prince's ritual magic or the tacit reign of the tactile? A saxophone barking in the distance, the stable measure of the foot replaced by seven-league boots. Fur-lined. Utilitarian delusions,[4] she cries, unusual effects, moss and oak leaves by the Roman temple, nest of nymphs and swimming moon, is it meaningful to assert geometrical diffidence?

1 raven more
2 too vast too barely blinking
3 possibly untitled
4 examples of

BOX CAMERA BOX

The film opens with bookstalls along the Seine (fig.13) and the spontaneous firing of neurons controlling face and tongue. Hippocrates knew it is in the brain that the dazzling white seafoam crystallizes into a pipe though the Ancients held that we ponder things in our heart. Solid bodies change little when subjected to subtitles, sound shifts, snow drifts—I mean, a ballerina is not just a metaphor.[1] Such slender projections, she moans, calligraphy, plaster lions, rhymes, crab canons.

The young man leafs through the books, with the smile of a fin-de-siècle soap bubble and cold feet. Even with skin flaunting its contacts, the brain is our messenger. Their relative stability is not ground enough for preferring solid bodies to the shape of thought.[2] Heard a call, she moans, vertigo, spasm, the milling crowd, cuts, angles, fleeting suddenly, dovecote, snowflakes, sprockets.

The still comes to life: a flock of pigeons bursts into flight toward Southeast Asia, while he punches his hand through the screen toward childhood.[3] Hippocrates came to his conclusions by listening to epileptics while the photographer folded his tripod. His overwhelming preference, though, was for solid bodies in vehement, shortlived motion. Vertigo, she moans, drop in temperature, alarm, loss of balance, feathers on the floor, words, foam on lips, no voice, book out of print.

The speed of stop-motion photography outstrips our most graphic expectations, yet it was in a sled, wrapped in fur, scared by the swift pace of the pony, that he had his first ejaculation. Epilepsy shows how the brain backstrokes against its own current. Even if color is solid it cannot equal a body in mute ecstatic abandon.[4] Towering firs, she moans, spirals, excess, last year's cuckoo, gold ring, ready-mades, left ear, tender tongue, tears, wide-open eyes, hypnotic, unreal.

1 engram of snow flat within the brain
2 that he, staring at
3 hilariously
4 the way to see me is to touch me

TOOL BOX

The gaze she knew even as a child envelops, the way velvet surrounds antlers in the period immediately preceding sexual aggression and mating. His attitude toward repetition casual—so many roses to suggest compulsion. But the definition[1] of terms like "attraction" or "palpable" depends on the enjambement of closed systems. The time you took, she wails, to open your arms, grow a beard, have rings under your eyes, wear a raincoat, swollen tongue, sigh, eyes downcast.

As a mature woman, Godiva knew all but one of her subjects would turn their eyes away from her humiliation, but my interest in the entire range of sexuality is genuine, quite genuine. If two or three cell bodies are gathered together they build suburbs of gray matter.[2] The whole system vibrates with red sky in progress, like sailor's delight minus part-time labor. Luminescence, she wails, mysteries, phenomena, sprouting likenesses, mirrors rampant, sunrise, porous color, out of phase gaze.

A naked little girl on a horse,[3] long tresses cover her body. My rash is now an unremovable garment covering my belly, buttocks, and genitals in a wet flush of color. Here lies the difficulty: a closed system can never be a mattress. My eyes, my voice, she wails, the deep spiral of the stairs, the small sea shell you'd brought me, snail house, bone color, sound in my ear.

A child Godiva would fulfill the most exhibitionist Emperor's fantasy, he of the New Clothes, but where is he? I found myself admiring the chocolate-colored trousers and yellow shirt which, irritating my gray matter, caused an explosion involving many cells at once, like lightning or an epileptic fit. And while physics does not explicitly define the body as rigid,[4] the whole system changed from rain to sleet. Panic, she wails, lilies made up yellow, garlands, wintergreen, palm leaves, seasonal emblems, splinter of red stone, open sky.

1 useful if inadequate
2 like chronic abnormalities that irritate
3 poorly fed
4 I'll never forget the mechanical chess player in his turban